Irish Elk and Other Extinctions

by

Christine Macfarlane

First published 2025 by The Hedgehog Poetry Press,

5 Coppack House, Churchill Avenue, Clevedon. BS21 6QW

www.hedgehogpress.co.uk

ISBN: 978-1-916830-45-5

Contents

START WITH KNOT

After Sarah Howe

not all instructions are straightforward
        enough confusion reigns to flood bubbling ditches

not every relationship ends in happy-ever-afters
        chimera, kaleidoscopes have short, bright moments

not all broadcloth is cut accordingly – much is done on the bias
        comfort may be gained from patchwork

not every stone is imbued with welcome
        though spirits of place may weep as you leave

not all outstretched hands offer friendship or help
        though many do

not all voices rise in a chorus of love and great amens
        yet the song of turtledoves soothes the soul

not all paths lead through Elysian Fields
        it is right and just to be left with risk

not any moment or day or year seems right for this or that
        clocks have no sense of time

not enough honeyed wine, silk or perfume flows
        life can be full of lukewarm tea

not enough kindness is conjured to untangle Ariadne's thread
        only love can weave a safety-net or harness

not much time is left to you
        ancient theories abound on the wisdom of cutting knots

DILEMMA

Today's a day like no other day,
sky so blue, blossom sings from the trees,
late February and it feels like May.

Beast from the East hit this time last year.
If temperatures rise more than two degrees
there'll be other weather extremes to fear.

I ignore bald patches left in the lawn,
scars that remain from last year's drought,
enjoy this sun, so unseasonably warm.

I put aside thoughts of mortality
count early bumblebees with relief.
(I've over-indulged such thoughts lately.)

I make a coffee, know this machine
with its plastic capsules should go –
great macchiato but can't call it *green*.

Can one person make a difference?
I have a list and cheer on the children,
the young are warriors in earth's defence.

Gas hobs are to be a thing of the past.
I try to imagine a world without gas hobs,
think – must try harder – as I strike a match.

LOST AND SAVED

Golden shovels: 1. From Losing a Language *by W S Merwin –*
final stanza: 'here are the extinct feathers/here is the rain we saw'

Lost

There's a sad litany of loss here.
Yangtze river dolphins are
gone. Little Mariana fruit bats, the
ivory-billed woodpecker, extinct.
What is left? Photographs, feathers.
I speak for creatures no longer here.
Nothing can replace them but it is
for us to haul others back from the
edge; restore land, sea and rain;
speak up, tell our children what we
did, how we failed, what we once saw.

2. From Gift *by Czeslaw Milosz –*
opening lines: 'A day so happy/fog lifted early/I worked in the garden'

Saved

It had become a
shipwreck of a day,
little left to rescue, so
I thought harder how to be happy.
From the window I saw how the fog,
thick all day, had almost lifted.
I'd risen too early.
Maybe there was still time. I
watched as a blackbird worked
through the tulgey, wet grass in
hope of worms. I put on the
old coat, joined her in the garden.

IRISH ELK

megaloceros giganteus

What did he think, the hunter who first saw you?
Was he stunned at your towering headgear? Antlers
wider than his cave. Did he fear your great height,
so much taller than himself? Perhaps he gave chase
but unable to outpace you, returned to his cave,
drew on the walls in ochre and charcoal, recorded
your red-gold hide, black collar and chinstrap,
dark hump on your withers – those vast antlers.

Did you starve trying to scavenge enough to regrow
the massive headpiece each year? A maladaptation?
Breeding females were thought to favour bucks with
widest horns. I picture a chase through dense woods
hear the crash and clatter, see branches fly before
your great head is locked tight among the trees;
hear bellows of pain, laboured breath as you strain,
struggle and die from exhaustion in pursuit of love.

I can only imagine your enormous elegance,
think of herds that ranged through thinly-wooded
grassland from Ireland to the shores of Lake Baikal,
stopping to graze the sedge, grass or browse on
leaves of spruce and willow. Winter, and your warm
breath melted the snow as you dug in search of food.
Your giant lips tore softly at spring herbs and flowers.
Now only your bones are left to wonder at.

MRS M CONSIDERS THE METAMORPHOSIS OF ODONATA

Mid-July - air over the pond is frantic with dragonflies,
spindle-thin damsel flies - crimson, turquoise, garnet.
Darters, chasers, hawkers - design classics - their form,
life-style, hardly changed in three hundred million years.

They've not always lived life in the sun; they're on the wing
for a short six weeks. No, they've had another, darker life
in the reedy margins of the pond. Eggs this female lays now,
so neatly tucked beneath the lily pads, will emerge as nymphs.

Nymph is a beautiful word but these are unattractive, six-legged,
miniature monsters - each a crawling savage - with a folding,
swift-moving labium, its lower jaw. This knife-fork-spoon-in-one
shoots out from under its head to pierce, grasp and devour prey.

I wonder about metamorphosis. Does that bright, airborne creature
look upon its last, cast exoskeleton, recognise it as a former self?
She may undergo up to fifteen of these changes - I try to imagine
so many stages of vulnerability, the exquisite relief of flight.

CURLEW

Pushing through trees, early, I see curlew
work through fresh mud on the estuary.
They dig deep, curved beaks like scythes.
Now they're off, legs stowed, they curl away,
carry their cries with them, carolling freedom.
Dun waders from a muddy creek transformed –
see – they soar like angels. My soul soars too.
This power to lift you is their gift. Accept it.
Listen, that song will fly you to wild places,
coast and high moorland. Places exposed to
sky, wind, the kind of aloneness that heals.
Unmissable, this call to rise. Their song,
strong enough to snatch you from low tide
until you're beside them, wing to wide wing.

THE LACK OF SNAILS,

particularly in areas of poor, sandy soil
mean that Dutch great tits and other
small birds lay eggs whose shells are thin,
porous and fragile with no colour spots.

In calcium-poor woodlands, female great tits
search hard for snails and in desperation eat
grit and sand. Some fail to lay, others produce
defective shells or eggs with no shell at all.

Birds that seem unaffected are those whose
territories overlap with picnic sites where
females may find fragments of chicken shell
from hard-boiled eggs left by picnickers.

Intriguingly, pied flycatchers breeding in the
same woods produce normal shells but these
birds hunt out millipedes and woodlice – such
insects have exoskeletons rich in calcium.
Why great tits do not do this also, is unclear.

Note: From The Most Perfect Thing (Inside and Outside a Bird's Egg) by Tim Birkhead
(Bloomsbury, 2016)

THE SISTERS OF IMMACULATE HEALTH

Sister Ofelia leaves the chapel. The aquarium air is calm, cool.
Bubbles rise through well-water, music to displace *Salve Regina*
still percolating through her head. She puts on latex gloves and
watches the creature that stares through the glass of his tank.
Here is another of His mysteries.

The salamander's wide mouth makes a permanent smile.
Purple, feathered gills on his pale green head wave at her
like crazy water antlers. She thinks that he looks like
a diminutive Aztec god, yes, the wicked twin of Quetzalcoatl
and he has his own litany:

Achoque, grinning water god,
you wear these gills for life.
Doomed to be forever young,
Peter Pan of amphibians,
white mouse too, with unique
powers of regeneration.
Achoque, local axolotl,
journalists photograph you,
scientists study you, learn how
you regrow a severed limb,
rebuild your damaged organs.
Salamander, key to our elixir,
a secret recipe, bottled here.
Achoque, we will tend you.
From the polluted waters of
Lake Patzcuaro you came,
found sanctuary with us.
We are gentle, know your ways.
Here, you breed and thrive,
provide this remedy to soothe
coughs and bronchial insults.
Help us regenerate hope.

Note: Dominican nuns in Mexico successfully breed salamanders (Achoque), make an elixir for common ailments, and save them from extinction. New Scientist: June 2018; BBC World Service: Discovery; BBC Radio 4, October 8th, 2018

ANCHORITE

Snail glides, self-contained on her shining path.
Not for her some stone-walled enclosure but
as part of her slow, deliberate self,
she wears a helical cell, made-to-measure.
Eyes aloft, she's off on another pilgrimage,
mindful of every leaf and blade of grass.
From time to time she'll pause for reflection,
retreat, immured in her nacreous shell
or seek safe shade at the foot of a hedge
for a damp coupling with brother or sister
(each snail can be the one or the other).
But hermit life is the habit of her kind,
nomad member of a silent order.
Who can hear her prayers, guess her visions?

LOBSTER FISHING

On a soft, quiet day, late in the year,
leaves fallen, sap low, he cuts lengths of *Salix,*
black maul, osier, purple willow.

Through winter nights he bends the supple stalks,
deftly weaves them into lobster pots –
few have this art he learned from his father.

From the base each cane arches up and through
making a trap – two parts built as one –
the *kitchen* will hold a tasty bait

and in the *parlour,* lobsters will wait for the
slow thrum-thrum of his boat above them.
He stacks his pots in the sail loft, waits for better weather.

One spring morning, the sea a mirror to the risen sun,
he loads the *Puffin* with his traps, each pot
looped to a rope on deck, ready to splash over the side.

The put-put of his engine breaks the silence,
his boat carves the silver surface of the sea.
He steers at full tide to open water,

southward then, along the granite shore.
Below him weed and boulder, sunk-stone floors
tilt and shelve to dark-fringed places where lobsters lurk.

On he goes along this watery road.
Each dropped pot settles on the sea bed
and is mapped in his mind to a place on land.

Three days later when the squall has passed,
late sun setting fire to the wrinkled sea,
he heads out again, hoping for a catch.

The engine idles as he hauls the traps aboard.
He lifts a lobster from its willow cage,
blue coral-spotted carapace, wet and smooth.

SAVING PARADISE

There was a time I needed talismans
to conjure my paradise, pocket-sized
portkeys to carry with me: this piece of
driftwood, weirdly shaped, a black stone
tumbled smooth in the sea, the blue mug
from Trelowarren Pottery or my painting,
the church of St. Anthony-in-Meneage,
built near the beach among farm buildings.

Now I need nothing, I'm there in a snap,
smell the salt tang of half-dried bladder-wrack;
feel that sting of sand in a south east wind
as the tide turns to fill the creek. I walk from
Manaccan, down past Roscaddon and on
through the woods to Gillan. A narrow path
leads under sweet chestnut and sessile oak
along the creek-side. And as I go on,

I hear curlews cry, low, slow at first, then
higher, faster as they rise, take their voices
with them, leave the mud and rag-worm
to sanderling and oyster catcher. Sun
skitters off the water. On the far bank,
no sign of human life. Timeless. Could be
prehistory, until the white farmhouse,
a concrete slipway and an upturned boat.

I sit on a wooden bench, *In memory of John,*
who loved this place and messing about in boats,
cross The Green with its gypsy caravan
and I'm on the pebbled beach. A freshening
breeze has me full in the face as I turn,
look out to sea. Sheltered by a garden wall
an artist works, keen to capture this paradise
on canvas, the granite church, the boats, the sea.

THE DYING GAUL

A bronze statue, Iford Manor, Wiltshire

Here's a wooden door in the wall that surrounds a secret garden.
On top of the lintel, leaning on his upturned shield,
sits a life-sized, bronze Celtic warrior, dying.
Mortally wounded by some Roman soldier,
he's put aside his curved trumpet and sword belt.

Yet why would anyone want to place him here
to gaze in his last moments, not over a wide
landscape – maybe his battleground – or on the
shore of a quiet lake to sleep out his eternity,
but overlooking a steep, narrow country lane?

His head droops, his sad face looks down forever on passers-by.
Maybe he sees the snowdrops and pale crocus that grow here.
If he could raise his neck enough to turn his head
he would see what he must have heard through decades –
the noise of a river as it flows through the valley below.

Walk past the fallen warrior and follow that sound.
Soon there's a double-arched bridge that splits
the fast-moving current and at the centre
like the figurehead of some land-locked stone ship,
stands Britannia. Her trident is lost but she steadies her shield.

If she looks up to her left she must see him dying and dying.
Perhaps she has his back as she faces upstream.

TALKING OF DEATH

We never had a name for it.
I thought I didn't care where my bones would lie,
now cemeteries seem like small acts of enclosure.
Headstones stand in a misery of rain,
tell of life as a past instalment, while
in the dim church, thin organ music
lifts hymns to a timbered roof.
No – when I'm dead and beyond description,
go out, a hatless mourner, as the year
gives in to autumn. Stand on some bridge
and watch the movement of water below.
It's not from earth we came but from the sea.
Scatter my dust in that fast-flowing stream,
know that the river will carry me home.

SECOND THOUGHTS

A re-cycling lorry backs into the close,
takes plastic, cardboard, tin and paper – destined for
reincarnation as furniture, car-parts, packaging, clothes.

At the charity shop I wonder who wore these shoes;
could I walk a mile in them, share that intimacy?

You can buy a past in here, I think; a past with melancholy;
items cherished – to a point.
Then I think on – so often told how I was born pre-loved.

JOSEPH WRIGHT IN CONVERSATION WITH ADMIRERS AT AN EXHIBITION

After An Experiment on a Bird in the Air Pump *by artist Joseph Wright of Derby, 1768*

Light is the thing. It is the Age of Enlightenment after all.
Chiaroscuro, tenebrism, a tension between light and dark.
I play with light. If I get it right, I trick the canvas into life.
Where to place the light in the painting, that is crucial.

This scene is illuminated by a single light source. See how
I have put the candle-lamp low on this table, round which
friends have gathered this evening. It up-lights their faces,
picks out each crease and fold in their clothes but leaves

the rest of the room in different, intimate, depths of shadow.
Polished objects gleam. See how the table surface reflects
the girls' clothing, the spectacles in Darwin's hand and the
partially-inflated bladder in that specimen glass.

Darwin looks serious, perhaps thinks of our changing times?
Light is reflected too, from the philosopher's air-pump.
(I call my central figure 'philosopher' – his dress, wild hair).
He is both thinker and entertainer, though he must see

how alchemy gives way to the new discipline of science
(Darwin's ahead of him there). The old man challenges. See
his hand thrusts forward, his eyes draw you in to the scene.
He asks, *And what of this bird? Shall I finally suffocate it?*

They all know he has the power to do this, his right hand
hovers on the lid of the jar. The father, conflicted, comforts
his daughters yet urges them to watch. The boy opposite
is keen as mustard. His uncle keeps note of the time.

The young lovers care for nothing but each other.
Behind them all, a family servant lowers the bird cage.
To receive the reprieved creature? Or does he let it linger
between shelf and table to tease, add to the tension?

Was it always so, Mr Wright, our response to dark and light?
Will it always be like this? Maybe the philosopher sees
further than we think. And what of the moon?

RAINDROP

I'm watching raindrops line up on a wire fence.
A necklace of water-beads, every tiny orb reflects

refracts the light – each sparkles, dazzles for a moment,
drops and is lost in the grass, soaks into the earth.

And this observation is not just about raindrops but about
the nature of water, each bead a distillation of ditch, river, sea.

They rise as vapour, condense from clouds to fall again,
to water the land, to fill the ditch, river, sea.

So this poem is about the cyclical nature of life and love. How
inevitable it is to rise and fall, to become, to shine, to be lost.

LETTER FROM THE MOON

I rake my patch of ragolith – moon soil
has the texture of snow, smells of cordite.
We wondered if anything could grow here
but there are glass roses, rubidiums,
heleniums, my favourite moon daisies –
all brittle, fragile things. They have petals,
not in the way we understand *petal*
(soft, fragrant), but they display certain style
and they are proof against the endless sun.

At this time of lunar day, I sit above
Mare Serenitatis, watch our home planet
move across the dark of space. Ever-bright
jewel, all blue and green, and white with
cloud and snow. I long for cloud and snow.
At night, necklaces of light, strung across
the world, blink and wink at me. How this moon
pulls and orders earth's vast tides, whilst here
every drop of water is hard won –

finite volumes irrigate our hydroponic farm.
We few scientists graze on lettuce like aphids.
I think of the nights we stood in our own garden,
gazed up at this magical moon. And though
I ache for you to sit beside me – no grass,
though you might admire my cut-glass flowers –
not two hundred and forty thousand miles away,
but I couldn't bear to uproot you. So do this:
put your hand on the damp earth, think of me.

O POLAR ICE CAP,

great Arctic waste, that never wasted a thing,
        stop us.
Call time on our grubby exploitation.
We couldn't resist the desire to come and take a look at you.
And blown away by your harsh, wild beauty,
your open, diamond-dazzle spaces, we did what we always do
(with our degenerate need to dominate) we sent in more men.
Men with anoraks and black goggles against your glare,
turned sleds into whining jet-skis,
revealed our 'geographical curiosity' as a
        dirty grab for oil.
Now ice-shelves for nursing seal and resting walrus are lost,
melted away in all our self-polluted, hot air.
Polar bears have become scavengers for scraps in dustbins,
swim for miles, their hunt a hunt for solid sea-ice
while you painfully give birth to giant calves of glacier.
May your moans and howls terrify the grasping life out of us.
O Ice-Mother, cold Snow Queen, ruler of frozen tundra,
don't let us near what's left of your whiteness, we *will* smirch it,
have our wicked way with you, whatever the cost.
O conjure a freezing fog; whip up a piteraq and let it blow for weeks.
Usher in a new ice-age.
Freeze us out.

Note: After Philip Gross, Moon, O

REQUIEM FOR A GLACIER

Dawn comes with grey light and promises.
You sit with your notebook and write in hope. You do.
But haunted by news, you rehearse the litany of misery,
think, *write yourself out of this, if you see a way through.*
Yet each day brings more. Disasters. Extinctions.

Glacier: vast body of ice able to move under its own weight.
Okjokull lived seven hundred years in the mouth of a volcano;
there, people gather to mark the passing of an ice giant.
It's officially dead. And in its wake, this patch of snow,
a pale smudge across black basalt. As for the funeral party,

if we are human, we are guilty, not least because of our number.
Fires burn Australia and we wonder if the planet's beyond repair.
There, the thin, cold air makes it painful for mourners to breathe.
Do they think of the innocent, of children, the unborn – or a bear,
further north near Svalbard maybe, stranded on fragile ice?

Above the laments of anoraked backpackers, a clear Icelandic sky.
Arctic tern (sea swallows) pass far above on some migratory path.
Where are the grown-ups, the wise? Are they quite vanquished?
Some heads lift to scan the sky. Not quite ready to give up faith,
they search for that one bird with a twig in its blood-red beak.

ACKNOWLEDGEMENTS

Acknowledgements are due to following publications and their editors, in which some of these poems, or versions of them first appeared: *Anchorite* in *Caduceus* issue 109 (and commended in Troubadour International poetry Competition 2020); *Letter From the Moon* in *The Rialto* issue 90 (and commended in Nature and Place Prize 2020).